MAPPING
THE MIND

THE ART OF SKYRUNNING UK

MAPPING

THE ART OF SKYRUNNING UK

THE MIND

A GUIDED SERIES

JOHN
PROCTOR

MAPPING
THE ART OF SKYRUNNING UK
THE MIND

Copyright © John Proctor 2021.
Foreword Copyright © Jon Bracey 2021.

John Proctor has asserted his right under the Copyright, Designs and Patents Act 1988 to be identified as the author of this work.

Ⓓ Design and layout by Ryder Design – *www.ryderdesign.studio*
Illustrations © John Proctor and Becky James.

A CIP catalogue record for this book is available from the British Library.
ISBN 978-1-5272-9553-7

Front cover top photo: Charlie Proctor. Front cover bottom photo: John Proctor.

Every effort has been made to achieve accuracy of the information in this guidebook. The authors, publishers and copyright owners can take no responsibility for: loss or injury (including fatal) to persons; loss or damage to property or equipment; trespass, irresponsible behaviour or any other mishap that may be suffered as a result of following the route descriptions or advice offered in this guidebook. The inclusion of a track or path as part of a route, or otherwise recommended, in this guidebook does not guarantee that the track or path will remain a right of way. If conflict with landowners arises we advise that you act politely and leave by the shortest route available. If the matter needs to be taken further then please take it up with the relevant authority. Users should always be aware of weather forecasts, conditions, time of day and their own ability before venturing out.

John proctor below the mighty North Face of Ben Nevis. **Photo**: John Proctor.

'It was a privilege to organise the first Skyrunning race in
the UK, and later host the Skyrunning World Championships
at Skyline Scotland in 2018. Skyrunning events differ greatly
from one country to the next, and from one race to another.
What all Skyraces have in common though, is a great
sense of adventure in the mountains requiring plenty
of physical fitness and nerve. This collection of routes
is a fantastic way to inspire DIY adventures.
Be safe and have fun!'

Shane Ohly – Race Director of Skyline Scotland

Contents

John Proctor enjoying the exposure on Bristly ridge in the Ogwen Valley. **Photo**: Charlie Proctor.

Acknowledgements

The opportunity for creating this book came from a difficult year of Covid lockdowns and the need to think creatively when the outdoor industry I've worked in for 30 years was hit hard. I also reached the ripe old age of 50 which fuelled the ambition to write a guidebook to help others experience the buzz of Skyrunning.

The friendships and experiences I have gained through adventures and working in the outdoors, have given me the knowledge and skills to move amongst the mountains. There are so many people who have helped shaped this and I owe them all my thanks, but more recently certain folk particularly stand out as being supportive and encouraging.

Bernadette Cook introduced me to Skyrunning, and the mighty Majka Bajka pushed me at pace through long, high mountain days. Rob Stevenson and Shaun Denham kept the momentum for local runs. Richard Allen and Graham Tiffany were great company for the many weekends in the mountains – both running and climbing.

Lyndon Chatting-Walters and Chloe Wilson need mention for their friendship and support throughout the lockdowns. Becky James for encouraging me to approach Nathan Ryder – the designer who has made this guidebook into a professional product.

Finally, thanks to Anna – my wife, running and climbing partner, who understands my need for long hours on the mountain in all weathers and for never showing doubt or stress.

John Proctor on the final Summit. **Photo**: Chloe Wilson.

John Proctor competing in the Glencoe Skyline race. **Artist**: Clarke Butler.

Foreword

John's raw passion, endless enthusiasm, and thirst for adventure come across in spades. Skyrunning is the dark art of combining fell running with technical scrambling, and even moderate climbing. Demanding an array of skills, these committing pursuits can give a unique sense of freedom, etching vivid memories into our minds.

This is no glossy edition full of staged photographs. It's a no frills, down to earth, and humble guide. Very much in keeping with John's own approach to life. However, it's extremely well researched, and packed full of original and inspiring adventures.

Whether you're a seasoned fell runner, rock climber, or new to running in the hills of the British Isles I guarantee you'll soon be reaching for the OS maps to plan your first skyrunning mission.

Jon Bracey – Alpinist, Skyrunner and IFMGA Mountain Guide

Introduction

Welcome to *Mapping the Mind: The Art of Skyrunning*, a complete UK series. The United Kingdom celebrates its wildly spectacular, richly varied and easily accessible mountain landscapes. Sculptured and battered by the extremes of weather and time, they have been mapped by our forebears and are now enjoyed by such as us: modern-day athletes in pursuit of adventure.

These rugged mountains – with their trails, cliffs, ridges, rivers and valleys – lure the adventure athlete away from the norms and constraints of everyday life, to run, climb, swim and walk amongst them; for the seeker of fun, adventure and challenge, epic and everlasting experiences await.

To fully embrace these experiences, the athlete must train hard, learn, develop new skills and, above all, desire, dream and be committed. Personal reward and strength emerge from perseverance, and the determination to push on deep into your very soul in the pursuit of your dream. The joy attained from your experiences is the only reward; memories etched into your mind the only trace of your path. It is because of this passion for the mountain experience that many runners and climbers turn to skyrunning.

Skyrunning – the name given to running/climbing high upon an extremely technical trail – requires a great degree of personal skill and knowledge, and can place huge physical and mental demands on us. There is risk and uncertainty, and the sport calls for huge commitment: these are the hallmarks of adventure; in order to succeed, athletes require passion, inner strength and dedication: the hallmarks of the adventurer.

Mapping the Mind is a series of descriptive sky runs; its aim is to guide you, and to develop your skills and knowledge as your heart, legs and lungs grow stronger, and you run and climb your way through mainland Britain's wildest and highest mountain peaks.

Over the past four years I have completed each of the routes in this series, logging the memories and 'mapping my mind'. It is from the wellspring of these memories that I give to you the adventure of skyrunning UK – a series to challenge and excite.

Artist: Becky James

Anna Proctor and Chloe Wilson enjoying the last rays. **Photo**: John proctor.

Personal acceptance

Running and climbing in the mountains brings with it a high level of personal challenge and risk; it is your right to take these risks and your responsibility to accept them.

I hope you see and feel a sense of the 'Old School' in the words of this guide, using the descriptions to plan runs and create memories. Leave the technology in the bag, along with all the inner chatter and dialogue from our modern lives. Have tech with you if you need to – a phone in the bag tracking your movements is okay, and a GPS on standby in case of absolute emergency is a good idea... But! If you are trusting these devices to navigate your way around the mountain, then this series is not for you.

This guide aims to develop the big mountain picture within your mind: a picture or panorama which reflects you – your thoughts, knowledge, capabilities and understanding of yourself.

Your reflection could be composed of years of mountain journeys, or you could be looking forward to taking your first steps on a high mountain trail. Every time we step onto the mountain, focus, caution and desire should lead us. Mishaps along the way could cost dearly, no matter who we are.

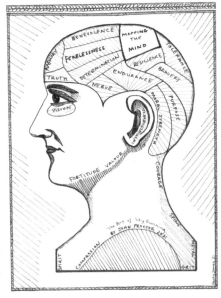

Artist: Becky James

Ensure you train and learn through study and hard work; accept help, be inquisitive and share experiences, knowledge and skills with other athletes of all abilities. In this way we not only develop ourselves, but also contribute to the community of high adventurers who surround us with inspiration and joy, for we are nothing without those around us.

The knowledge in this guide comes from my own personal and love-filled reflections, memories of the mountain and knowledge developed from a 30-year career working as an outdoor pursuits instructor – thirty years of backpacking, running and climbing with others, having fun whilst growing stronger both in body and mind. I owe my companions so much, for their friendships have enriched my life far beyond my dreams and expectations.

Being a Yorkshireman has had its challenges when translating memories into intelligible English! I can assure you I've had this guide edited.

I've also taken every effort to maintain an accurate and detailed description of each route within this guide. All the distances and height measurements are taken from my own personal running app recordings. Route times are set to allow for all weather conditions on the mountain and taken from my own pace. You must record your own times and use them as your guide.

I expect anyone who is to use this guide to accept the risks involved with skyrunning – there are many to consider.

Have fun with every step you take. Be strong.

John Proctor

Striding for the Ultra

There are 17 skyrunning routes detailed in this guide across 3 mountain areas: The Lake District, Wales and Scotland.

- (I) – 6 introductory skyruns (12–20km)
- (M) – 6 mid distance skyruns (24–28km)
- (U) – 3 sky Ultras (45–58km)
- (B) – 2 bonus runs

These routes can be regarded as a series where you progress from the introductory runs, onto the mid distance runs and finally tackle the sky Ultra. Following the series will help develop your skills for mapping the route to your mind; this is essential for efficient running and navigation whilst focusing on the route. You should develop your running style, rock scrambling ability, mental / physical strength and equipment needs, as detailed in the skills set section that follows. As you move beyond the introductory runs, you should pay more attention to your fuel and hydration needs. You should also build up a picture of who you are; your strengths, skills and skyrunning knowledge. Each run will allow you to review your progress and assess areas that need improvement. Bringing together all your skills and knowledge, to accept the challenge of the sky Ultras and complete this skyrunning series

The 2 bonus runs are in addition to the series and offer another ultra and a vertical 4000m ascent; both are tests of endurance, and great fun.

Big picture, route planning and preparation

How to use this guide

Once you have decided to try one of the skyruns in this guide, the planning process of relating the detailed description to a paper map should begin.

First, lay the relevant map out on a table or floor and use the provided descriptions to follow the route around the map (use a highlighter to mark the route, if it helps you to retrace it).

Next, use a magnifying lens (there should be one on your compass) to follow the line of the route, paying close attention to the contour lines and features, and pausing to focus especially on the technical parts of the trail. Break the route down into sections and gain more information on rock scrambles and ridges by reading guidebooks to complement this process.

Following this procedure will allow you to build a picture of the journey along the trail, from the start to the finish. Take your time to recognise the terrain and each of the different aspects of the sky run:

- What are my main big location features on this route?
  Take note of lakes, hilltops, big tracks, wall junctions, etc.

- Steep ascents – uphill technique required,
  begin the breathing technique.

- Steep descents – turn off the brain, engage the downhill technique.

- Where does the gully start and finish?

- How technical and exposed is the ridge? What time of day will we be running it? Will it be wet, and how strong will the forecasted wind be at that time of day? (More on weather forecasting in the next chapter.)

- Where does the rock scramble start? Do I have knowledge of the scramble? Have I read through the description in the scrambles guide? What is my climbing technique? Do I need my helmet?

- Where can we collect fresh water?

- Where can we cool off – next to a lake or waterfall?

- Where are the cafes, pubs or shops for a deserved break? Remember, it's a day out – on a long trail, if I drop down into a valley I like to stop for a meal in the pub, or sit on the top of Snowdon eating a warm pasty bought from the train station, before setting off into further reaches of the sky run.

- Where are the escape routes down to the valleys? Is there a place of shelter down there?

This process can take as long as you like; you may want to revisit the map many times, transferring your thoughts into memory. A few days before your skyrun date, when you feel you have memorised the route and all its challenges; then it's time to sketch.

Creating your sketch map

Now try sketching the route out: do this by hand and from memory, either on a piece of paper or on a computer.

Points to remember:
- Try to orientate the map.

- Place your reference points for the main trail features, and use symbols for the skyrunning skills and techniques.

- It doesn't need to be to scale.

- Remember it's a sketch, there is no need to spend all night on it – take 45 minutes to an hour at the most.

- If, after reflection, you're unhappy with your sketch, think about the route, reference the actual map, and try again.

Actual on route knowledge can only be gained by being on the mountain. The sketch is one part of the big picture build-up happening within your mind. As you make your way through the sky runs, and as the kilometres dissolve into your legs and lungs, the focused decisions you make, whether right or wrong, will become etched onto your mind map, building knowledge through experience.

Sketch maps are used to complement the route descriptions within this guide, and as you can see, they are rough sketches. Their purpose is to help you etch the route into memory, and assist with the planning process by developing a deeper understanding of the day ahead and the demands it will exert. **>>**

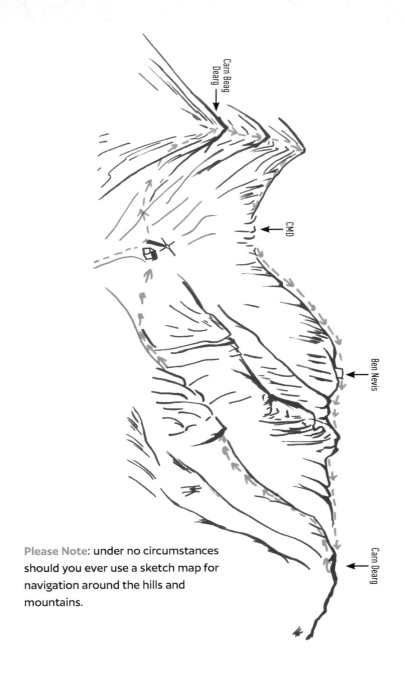

Carn Beag
Dearg

CMD

Ben Nevis

Carn Dearg

Please Note: under no circumstances should you ever use a sketch map for navigation around the hills and mountains.

Whatever the weather

What does the forecast say: how will it affect your planning, and ultimately your experience, whilst on the sky run?

On hot sunny days, I'll take every possible chance to cool down by soaking my lightweight hoody in a stream or lake and wearing it soaked whilst I run.

Heat exhaustion is a real threat; there's no shade on the high mountains.

In the winter months I'll carry a large synthetic jacket and winter mittens, which will help protect me from the foul, cold wet weather, along with extra food, a survival bag and maybe a flask of warm soup.

In pouring rain and strong winds (which is the worst of all conditions) I'll run in a heavyweight mountain jacket and carry a mid-weight synthetic jacket for when the water penetrates and the cold damp begins.

Whatever the weather, your safety and health is always paramount. By gaining awareness of the weather you can judge the conditions on the mountain. Heat, wind, cold and rain will affect your physical condition and your ability to keep pushing on and maintain focus.

Exhaustion can creep in on a long day in the mountains; all the elements of weather can add up.

Never go **unprepared**!

Weather forecasting

www.metcheck.co.uk
www.mwis.org.uk (Mountain Weather Information Service)
www.yr.no

All the above websites provide good mountain forecasts, and I will consult at least two of them when I'm in the planning process. Some sources provide visual images, which I find help with my mind mapping and therefore with development of the pre-run big picture.

What information am I looking for, and why? My main consideration here is to decide how the weather will affect my day. So, I'm looking for information on the following:

Wind speed and direction: could the wind affect my ridge running? How cold will the wind chill be, and will it drive the heavy rain into my face?

Cloud cover and height: low cloud means not only will there be no views but you will need more focused navigation. My map and compass may never leave my hand, and I might need to pace myself so that I can judge distance. Trying to run on the tops at night in the driving wind, rain and mist is not a good place to be. On a long day I will make sure I'm out of that zone by nightfall.

Amount of rain or snowfall: heavy rain means slippery rocks and trail, and every foot placement will require your full attention during the whole run. Ridges and rock faces will call for either absolute focus or the search for an alternative track in order to bypass them. Outdoor clothing will fail and the cold wet will creep through and begin to sap your strength. Streams and rivers will swell and become hazardous to cross. Snow on the ground will mean extra clothing, different running shoes, ice axe, and spikes or crampons.

Soft snow can cause more hazards, while good hard snow usually means fast flowing movement.

Being out in all weather is a requirement if you want to become fit and strong, and build up your mind map. Trail knowledge acquired through focused decision making and experiencing the full effects of nature on the mountain is not only an incredible feeling, but will contribute to building your inner strength and understanding of your capabilities.

Don't go **unprepared**!

Skye ridge, Anna Proctor. **Photo**: John Proctor.

Anna Proctor on the Ring of Steall. **Photo**: John Proctor.

Personal equipment

Your choice

Only spending time on the mountain will make your kit personal. There is a huge range of equipment to choose from, and specialist product development combined with the growing adventure athlete market have led to the creation of boutique-style shops. Sales in this year's colours, and brands promoted by sponsored heroes drive this development, and there is a wealth of opinion on products. Having the right equipment is a privilege and whilst money can buy this privilege it is not as important as being out running on the trail. Putting the miles into your legs is key to skyline running. It's also where your cash should be going!

I was impressed by some alpinists from South America, who I met and chatted with below the north pillar of Mount Fitz Roy in Patagonia. They had one ice axe between the three of them and no crampons on their trainers, whilst we Western alpinists had all the gear and four ice axes between the two of us. I was full of admiration, watching their companionship and progress over the glacier and onto the immense wall of golden granite, their calm focused approach carrying them up the mountain – an amazing sight.

Wearing all the gear no doubt looks good in your selfies but, if you want real memories, aim for more 'likes' on your running app: this is one of the only tech toys to get a place on my kit list, and is a great way to add to the big picture by creating a collection of data both from days out and your local training runs.

When stepping up to skyrunning you may need to invest in some new equipment, but sift carefully through the choices and spend well. You will find no sponsored product placement in this guide, only my list of recommended essentials.

A suggested list of equipment for skyrunning

- trail shoes/boots with a good grip for mountain running: 5mm lugs on the sole of the shoe is recommended in most situations
- running shorts, leggings
- sport vests, t-shirt, and windproof hoody
- synthetic gilet or body warmer
- spare lightweight weather resistant jacket/smock
- mid-weight synthetic mountain jacket
- waterproof jacket with underarm zips and storm hood
- heavyweight synthetic winter storm jacket
- super-light waterproof trousers
- hat, beanie, headband
- sunglasses
- neck gaiter/buff/beanie
- thin gloves, over-mittens
- head torch with substantial beam and durability
- survival bivvy bag
- water bottles
- running vest/pack
- compass with large magnifying lens
- map

Please note, I do not recommend running poles for skyrunning: if stored away on the front of the vest when climbing, they can hinder upper body climbing movement, affecting both flow and concentration.

The big picture you've been developing will guide your equipment requirements and choices. Packing your running vest or backpack may take a few attempts while you grapple with decisions; lay out all you require and check it once more, questioning its use before it goes in the bag. Fast and light may sound good, but when you have a long day of skyrunning ahead of you, don't go out under-equipped. A little extra weight in the pack may well be worth the effort, bringing you extra comfort if conditions become difficult.

Skill sets

Mental strength/mindset

A high level of mental and physical strength is required for skyrunning; the mind is, without doubt, our most powerful tool, and learning how to focus your mental resources whilst under a sustained bombardment of chatter from your inner mind is the number one skill. Even a shadow of doubt can smother your psyche, affecting your thoughts and ambitions. You can improve your performance by learning about the workings of the inner mind in this way. Personal growth and knowledge can be developed through conscious choices: accept and embrace all your experiences for what they are, a day out in the mountains. There are many books available to assist with mental training, so do your research, choose, and begin learning.

The following is a word on mindset from my friend, and an ex-pro boxer:

'I'm Rob Stevenson and for ten years I was a professional boxer contending in over fifty fights. The main thing I learnt along the way is this: you can strive to be as physically fit as you deem possible, but if you have not prepared yourself mentally for whatever challenge lies ahead, then the level of success you are craving will almost definitely be harder to achieve. A mindset of 'I can and will' is paramount towards your success or your goals. Boxing is one of the hardest sports – when you are at the point of physical exhaustion, you then

must cope with an opponent who is trying to knock you out. The real battle is always the mind over the body. Be Strong' – **Rob Stevenson**

An important mindset to adopt towards any sky run is to take a flexible approach: the end game is to return home. The mountain is not trying to kill you!

Breathing

Understanding how to breathe is another powerful skill for the skyrunner. Apart from integrating your mind and body, it helps to oxygenate the blood flow to your legs, reducing lactic acid and carbon dioxide, and can help to reduce stress and anxiety. Developing a focused breathing technique will allow you to go further and faster (do your research well).

Running posture/technique

A skyrunner needs many running techniques; learn about these, develop your own style and you'll enjoy relaxed fast flow over all mountain terrain. Areas to consider include:

- uphill running
- descents

Ridge running

Focus on what the trail demands and on how you adjust your posture and running style. This will allow you to push through the difficult hours when you are tired, and your running style changes because of the aches and pains of the day. Poor running style and loss of focus can lead to injury –

a twisted ankle, which is not only painful but can lead you to suffer from exposure high on the mountain. The flow of movement will come through focused and dedicated training runs, and through personal study utilising online learning, specialist books, or, possibly, a running coach.

Rock climbing and scrambling

The scrambles in this guide provide the skyrunner with steep and exposed climbing. Swift movement can be achieved by focused dedication to climbing-specific training. You can learn good techniques from a climbing coach and self-coaching guides. The ridges and scrambles are worth a pre-run visit to develop your mind map, and build confidence, technique and strength.

Map reading

Why use a paper map and compass? Relating the map to the ground and having the confidence to follow your compass bearing is not only a key skill but is essential to your survival on the mountain. Only through spending time on the trail can you truly develop this. Focused navigational decisions made whilst out on the terrain, implant memories, extending the depth of your trail knowledge – a knowledge you will need if you are to complete all the skyline runs in this guide.

If you are looking to develop this key skill, there are many ways to do this:

- join a local orienteering club – orienteering is a perfect way to learn
- undertake a hills and skills course
- complete a national navigations award course

- hire a mountain leader for some hill skills coaching
- do an online course
- use a self-teach guide

Health and fitness

Home schooling, conditioning and strength

I'm a married man with two children and my own skyrunning story started and continues from my home city of Leeds, in West Yorkshire. My motivation to take up skyrunning evolved out of a love of alpine and winter climbing, both of which involved travelling to faraway destinations. Wonderful and exciting photos on the internet, and in glossy magazines and books drip-fed into dreams of gripping climbing adventures on granite walls and snow-capped mountains. The time constraints of being a family man meant that I was focused and ready for any trip away.

'Home schooling', to me, is about the desire to be a focused alpinist or climber, who is looking to the future for adventure through demanding and wild challenges. Building a big picture of experiences in faraway places helps to create memories of these adventures and build up the confidence to try more. My focus and commitment evolved over the years to the point where each summer I would focus on a trip to the Alps for a 'big wall' epic. Then as the autumn approached, I would switch my focus to hill running and enter the world-famous, annual Original Mountain Marathon, which would then lead into an epic season of winter climbing in Scotland.

I would usually make three journeys to the mountains throughout the year, and this required the development of different skill sets. Skyline running came to my attention along with the creation of the sky racing calendar, organised by the International Skyrunning Federation. All of these elements came into combination to create the prospect of epic adventures, through the art of skyrunning in the mountains. Once I became aware of this possibility and decided I wanted to try out this new challenge, my 'home schooling' began.

The curriculum

Local running:
- cross-country trails in local woods and moorlands, developing running techniques

- reps of hill routes and city steps, developing the legs, lungs and footwork

In the gym:
- four of the best, squats, clean and press, dead lift, calf raises and lunges – a programme for strength, stamina and power

- core, planks, t press-ups, dumbbell rows, kettlebell chops, kayakers, dips and TRX for all over iron strength

- bench press, lat machine pulldowns, curls - all for conditioning of the upper body

- fitness classes/circuit training

At home, in the garden be creative around the home to build a core and condition circuit; this can be difficult to fit in while you're doing everyday chores, but can be good for your mindset, helping you to drift away from the home and focus on adventure.

Local climbing

Indoor climbing centres and bouldering walls provide you with an excellent opportunity to improve your climbing movement technique, strength and fitness, and to develop a focused training regime in order to accomplish this.

Outdoor at the local crag, practice your movement – especially footwork – on boulders and rock climbs. Remember that the climbing on a sky run may be low in terms of grade, but you will not be tied to a rope: confidence must be derived from the skills you have developed – a misadventure whilst climbing high on the mountain can lead to severe personal harm.

Mixing it up

- morning run of 13km; lunch, then two to three hours bouldering; followed by early evening at home, working on core and conditioning

- rock climbing all day, strength training in the gym at night

- cycle to work and hit the gym on the way home

Building up athletic resilience through continued and varied all-day training sessions will give you the conditioning you need for the sustained physical effort it takes to run a skyline. Having the commitment to 'mix and match' is key to developing all over mental and physical strength. Allow your body and mind to soak up your time on the mountain and process that time into memories that will last a lifetime. Once you step-up to skyrunning and your training begins, consider putting a few 'mix and match sessions' in per week.

Injury prevention

I enjoy training so much that I find it easy to overdo it; however, I've learnt that my mind is much stronger than my body. A punishing training regime puts strain on your body which, whilst causing it to grow strong, can unfortunately sometimes break it. There will be hurt and pain as you grow into a skyrunner;

that pain is yours, so embrace it. I was once told: "pain goes away", but "pride is forever"; I would say that pain does fade, and it is the memories of epic adventure that last forever. Try leaving your pride at home and listen to your body, understand what its language is, as it speaks to you with niggles, swellings, bruises, aches and pains. Rest is key to building strength; remember this and factor it into your life. Remember, also, the following pointers:

- warm up – ten minutes is sufficient, but make it dynamic

- stretching – help boost your flexibility through both static and dynamic stretching, paying particular attention to the dynamic. This will improve your active flexibility, stimulating your central nervous system and blood flow to the muscles and tendons

- foam-roll – regular rolling is a key tool for keeping your legs going over many years and long distances. Work out the exercises and take the pain – it's yours

- running shoe insoles – if you can, find a good musculoskeletal podiatrist and invest in some carbon flexi type insoles: your shoe will then help to maintain the balance of skeletal mechanics ensuring your knees, hips and back last the distance. Note: they are expensive!

Food is fuel

Fuelling your run may require some thought, and in this area too there's a lot of information and opinion. I was always taught to 'keep the fire burning' so I pack lots of tasty, mini-snacks that I enjoy eating. I may stop at a café or pub and get a coffee, pasty or even a full plate of food if I'm doing a long slow run. I'm not trying to break any speed records, I'm just out to put some big distances into my legs. With this in mind, the overall experience I'm aiming for is that of a good day out in the mountains. However, if I step up a gear into a race pace, I will enter the 'march of death' at some point within the later stages of an 'Ultra'. This is admittedly a very uncomfortable way to finish the day and is an issue I have yet to crack.

Studying your nutrition and fuel is key to the success of any Ultra skyrunner, and as you will need to build up physical strength and develop endurance, you are going to require a significant energy input.

Hydration

The amount of water I carry will depend on the condition of the mountain: water can be in short supply if the mountain is either frozen, or dry from heat. Generally, I get all my water from streams, and carry extra capacity only when heading up high if I think there won't be a source on the tops. Making a note of the water sources on your runs will help you to develop the big picture when you plan for longer days. Understanding the condition of the mountain on those days will allow you a safer and stronger journey over them.

As with fuel, I drink little and often, and may add electrolytes and energy sources to my bottles.

Keeping your body fit and replenished throughout a long day requires a lot of focused implementation – something I find difficult to do when I'm on the mountain, navigating and negotiating my way.

Anna at the start of an early winter sky run. **Photo**: John Proctor.

England: Lake District Skyrunner

Welcome to the Lake District and the Lakeland skyrunner series – four sky runs to develop and challenge you. These routes in the sky take the runner through a panoramic series of breathtaking and beautifully harsh mountain terrain, shaped and battered over 450 million years through volcanic eruptions and the shifting of glaciers. Steep and technical ascents, long high trails over soaring skylines, and fast and free descents into deep, lush valleys are some of the fabulous features you will find here. To complete this series the runner must accept not only the mental and physical demands of the trail but also the ever-changing environment the Lake District weather throws at you. "If it's not raining, it's going to rain," is a common saying in the Lakes, so plan well! Committing to the sky intro and distance runs will help you to develop the big picture and ultimately lead you on to the Lakeland sky run Ultra.

Technical, exposed and demanding conditions are featured in the highlights of this series – the architecture of the rock, imposing and atmospheric, high on the north face of Pillar. You will experience ever-increasing exposure and views from Lord's Rake on Pavey Ark and the journey through the impressive high rock pillars of Scafell as you aim for the summit. This series delivers excitement and wonder as you travel through your skyrunning journey.

Lakes Skyrun. **Photo**: John Proctor.

Wasdale

Wasdale 11

11.6km | 1222m ascent | max elevation 969m | 2–4 hours

A short day through a big landscape, this is a steep and technical ascent **England's highest peak, featuring a focused, free and fast descent alon** **side Piers Gill – it has all the hallmarks of a quality sky run.**

The Skyrun

Travelling into Wasdale alongside Wast Water, the high mountain panoram opens up before your eyes. The National Trust car park at the top of Wa Water is the starting point for this run.

Begin with a good stride, heading east and following Lingmell Gill until you cro onto the steep climb of Brown Tongue. Continue towards Mickledore to th large boulder, study the screes below the three buttresses of Scafell Crag ar head into the Lord's Rake gully. You will encounter steep and loose scram bling until the West Wall Traverse appears. Head up through the amazir rock architecture, out of the gully and up to the summit of Scafell.

From the summit take the track towards Foxes Tarn (England's highest tar and the gully descent, which is steep and often flowing with water. Exit th gully below Broad Stand and head up the track through Mickledore to th summit of Scafell Pike (977m).

Head north-east towards Broad Crag and drop into the saddle via a short ar technical ridge descent. Continue the descent from the saddle north-west the head of Piers Gill. (This is a crossover point for the corridor route and link-up point for the distance and Ultra.)

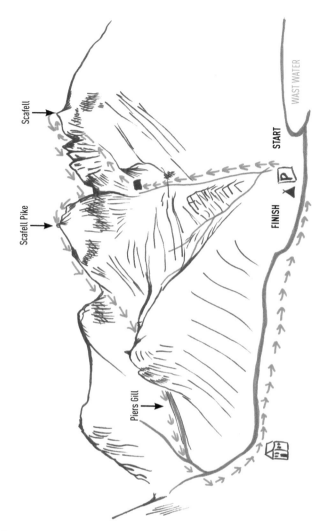

Continue the descent via the exposed mountain trail which descends alongside Piers Gill, hugging the clifftops and flirting with its edges, allowing you to appreciate the depth of this huge landscape feature. This section permits beautiful fast flowing running with some short downwards climbing. Descending all the way back into Wasdale, following the flow of the beck, there are plenty of opportunities to cool off and soak in its crystal waters.

Wasdale 20
20.4km | 2074m ascent | max elevation 893m | 4–6 hours

This route delivers technical running throughout the day, challenging ascents, exposed trails, tough steep descents, mind-bending rock features, and a high journey through Pillar's dramatic and exposed north face. A true line in the sky, this trail packs a punch and requires complete focus throughout.

The Skyrun

Begin the run in Wasdale, leaving your car at the village green parking area. Heading north-east begin the run with a steady trot up to Sty Head Pass. At the first aid box continue the climb by taking the track running north-west to the summit of Great Gable (899m).

From the summit continue, heading north-west for a steep and technical descent to the small tarn in the saddle at Beck Head. Heading west, climb the track to the first summit of Kirk Fell (786m), and continue on, following the old steel fence posts, past the small tarns to Kirk Fell summit (802m). Heading to the north, follow the fence post to a steep and technical (short downward climb) descent into the saddle at Black Sail Pass.

Continue heading west for about a kilometre until you see a small cairn above Green Cove. From the cairn, take the technical track heading below the massive north face to Robinson's Cairn (649m). From the cairn, head towards Pillar Rock and carefully navigate your way through the series of ledges and scrambles to the gap at the back of Pillar Rock, and then on to the summit of Pillar (853m). From the summit, head south-west to Scoat Fell (843m), which is a technical descent leading into classic ridge running. >>

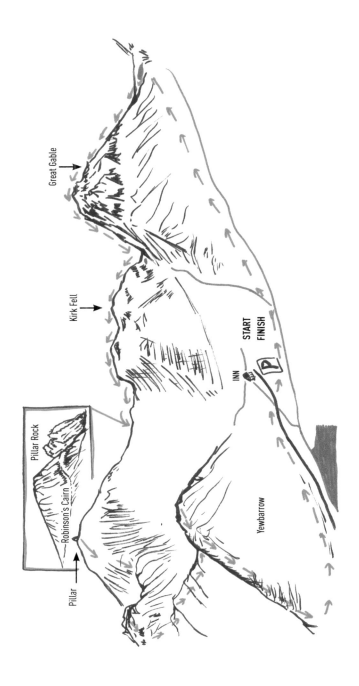

Great Gable

Kirk Fell

Pillar Rock

Robinson's Cairn

Pillar

INN

START
FINISH

Yewbarrow

Begin the long descent into Wasdale heading south-east over Red Pike (828m) to Dore Head (486m). This is fast and free running surrounded by an incredible panorama. From this point take the short scramble to the ridge of Yewbarrow (617m). Continue over the ridge, enjoying the views to the descent down Bell Rib – careful footwork and downward climbing bring you to the car park at Overbeck Bridge.

Head up the road back to your car.

 Wasdale Link-up

24km | **2892m ascent** | **max elevation 969m** | **6–8 hours**

You can link the Wasdale 11k with the Wasdale 20k via the corridor route link up point at the top of Piers Gill. From there, follow the corridor route north to Sty Head Pass, then pick up the trail heading to the summit of Great Gable

John Proctor descending clag in the west wall traverse Scafell. **Photo**: Chloe Wilson.

Langdale

Langdale 26

26.2km | 2247m ascent | max elevation 974m | 4–7 hours

Here, a 500m rock scramble from the valley floor to the first summit allows the runner access to this demanding trail, high above the valley floor. Focused navigation throughout is required to run this complex and beautiful route, which is a wild, exposed, fast and flowing mountain trail from the first to the last stride.

The Skyrun

The iconic silhouette of the Langdale Pikes attracts your eye as you drive into the valley and look for a space for your car. There are many places to park, and many visitors to fill the spaces, so an early departure is highly recommended for this route. The scramble up Stickle Ghyll and the path alongside can be gridlocked with people having fun and enjoying the easy access to this beautiful environment. I've selected the National Trust car park next to the New Dungeon Ghyll to start this run; however, you may need to park elsewhere, so feel free to start from a different point.

Begin by exiting the car park via the gate near the toilets, heading north-west. Within a few minutes you will hear the sound of Stickle Ghyll and reach the beginning of a very satisfying rock scramble which gives a fast ascent to Stickle Tarn. Follow the line of the Ghyll, staying close to its edges and scrambling up waterfalls and rock faces. This section is never difficult and continually interesting.

Above Stickle Tarn lies the impressive face of Pavey Ark and Jack's Rake, the continuation scramble taking you to the summit. Run around the tarn and

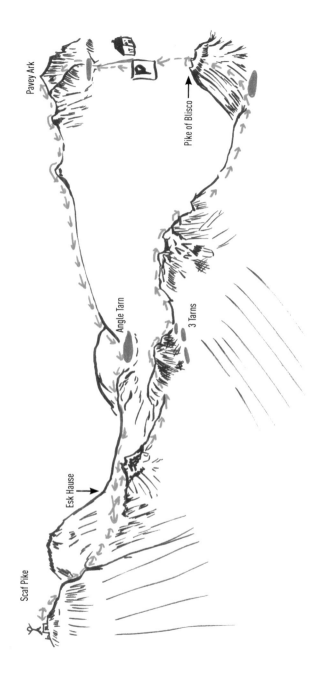

Pavey Ark

Pike of Blisco

Angle Tarn

3 Tarns

Esk Hause

Scaf Pike

begin your scramble. The demanding footwork and focused movement skills this calls for will reap the reward of increasing exposure and magnificent views as you ascend the Rake.

From the summit, head south-west to Harrison Stickle then west to Pike o Stickle. Continue north-west along the track over Martcrag Moor to Stake Pass. Head south-west, taking the trail to Angle Tarn. From the tarn, head up north-west to Esk Hause.

The track junction of Esk Hause has five trails leading away from it; the one heading south-east towards Esk Pike is the track to follow on the way back from Scafell Pike, so make a note for your return.

Take the trail heading west below Great End, steadily climbing to Broad Crag (934m), where you descend into the saddle below Scafell Pike (977m), and continue up the ridgeline towards the summit. Pay particular attention to the trail and create focus points along the way; in poor visibility your ability to move quickly across this technical terrain will depend on your memory of these points. This trail is also a link-up point for the Lakes Ultra.

From the summit of Scafell Pike head back north-east to Esk Hause and then south-east to Esk Pike (885m). Continuing to the south-east, drop down to the saddle – Ore Gap – and climb to the ridgeline of Bowfell (903m). Follow the ridgeline over Bowfell to the Three Tarns, taking in the views of Bowfell Buttress and the Langdale valley.

Heading south from the Three Tarns, scramble over Crinkle Crags keeping to the Langdale side for the short downward climb, and then on to the long, fast and free descent running east to Red Tarn. A final short climb up the trail to Pike of Blisco (705m) takes you to the final descent back into the Langdale valley to complete the run.

Anna Proctor and Chloe Wilson running fast and free. **Photo:** John Proctor.

Lakes Ultra Skyrun

50km | 3880m ascent | max elevation 973m | 10–14 hours

With this route, a full-scale epic adventure awaits the complete skyrunner. Feel the commitment, as this challenging journey unfolds within your inner mind. A high level of mental strength synced with physical prowess is the order of the day. This run demands focus, big picture awareness, and all the style and skills a skyrunner possesses. The runner must bring it all together, if they are to complete the Lakes Ultra.

The skyrun

This Ultra is a link-up of the Wasdale and Langdale routes. They are joined via the pass heading north-west from Angle Tarn to Sty Head Pass. This is enjoyable running on a good track.

Begin the run from the car park at the New Dungeon Ghyll hotel, where the path emerges straight into the rock scramble up the Ghyll, and goes around the lake and up Jack's Rake – a great warm up to begin the day. Follow the trail to Angel Tarn – initially fast and flowing running – then begin the digging in,

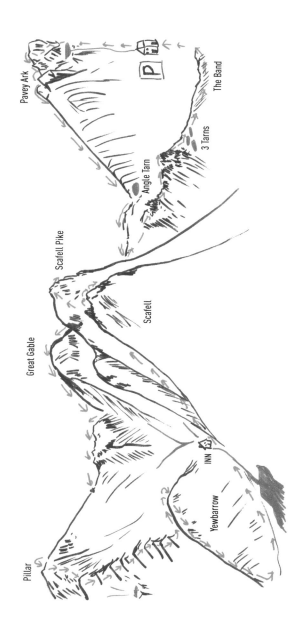

Pavey Ark

The Band

3 Tarns

Angle Tarn

Scafell Pike

Scafell

Great Gable

INN

Yewbarrow

Pillar

and pace yourself until the descent past the beautiful Sprinkling Tarn, which allows fast flowing running on to Sty Head Pass.

From the pass, head up and step into climb mode for the ascent of Great Gable; take no rest on the top, but head straight off into the descent, over Beck Head, and climb again to the summit of Kirk Fell and the technical descent to Black Sail Pass.

From the pass, head to Robinson's Cairn along the exposed and dramatic mountain trail on Pillar's north face. Good balance and an eye continuously focused on the route are required if you want fast flowing running. From Robinson's Cairn, head on up towards the summit of Pillar via the technical trail, ascending the ledges and terraces of the north face; enjoy the atmosphere surrounding this huge pillar of rock whilst keeping up your pace.

From the summit of Pillar step into downhill mode; a burst of steep technical descents accompany fast and flowing running, taking Scoat Fell, Red Pike and Yewbarrow in a blur of speed and control until you hit tarmac, and begin to head around the top of Wast Water. This is really cool running with awesome views of the surrounding peaks.

Breathe deep; this is an opportunity to refuel and hydrate as you head toward your ascent of England's highest peaks. The on-trail knowledge you have acquired will help your mindset as you prepare for maximum elevation topped with some steep and loose gullies.

Set your climbing legs to a pace and head on up towards the big boulder below Mickledore. Stepping on to the screes below the impressive rock architecture of Scafell Crag, you will find that an increase in focused footwork and route finding is required to navigate your way through Lord's Rake and the West Wall Traverse.

Exit the traverse onto Scafell and take in the summit before your descent via the Broad Stand gully; exit this and head over Mickledore and on to the summit of Scafell Pike. Maintain your focus for technical running and keen navigation as you run over Broad Crag and head towards Esk Hause. Once you have passed Broad Crag, enjoy the fast and flowing descent past Esk Hause and on to the final section of the run.

The short climb onto Esk Pike will help focus your mind and reset your pace for some good technical running. Maintain focus on navigation as you cross over Bowfell and drop down to the Three Tarns.

Heading east, begin your descent into the Langdale valley via the Band, a fast and free trail to ease your tired legs.

Majka Bajika on a winter lakes run. **Photo**: John Proctor.

The Scafell Leg Press

Bonus Skyrun

A 4k vertical day; five enduringly steep ascents; five incredibly fast and free descents. This run is great fun and brutally difficult from the first step away from your car. Don't be fooled by the apparent lack of commitment and distance in this run; this is a misconception which will only lead to your defeat! Be strong, stay focused and accept the full effect of the 4k day.

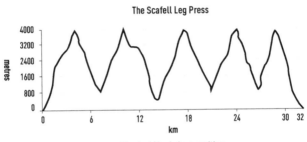

Warning! May induce vomiting

Begin the run at the National Trust car park situated at the top of Wast Water in Wasdale. Head up Scafell Pike via the west spur of Lingmell (807m) – this is a great warm up for the legs. Take note of the trail you cross, which comes from Wasdale Head, and head to Lingmell Gill as you begin the climb to the summit. From the summit of Lingmell continue your ascent of Scafell Pike.

There is no need to hang about on the summit, so descend via the ridge running north-east to the saddle below Broad Stand, then head north-west down to Piers Gill, and continue following Piers Gill via the trail, running along its edges until its water filters into Lingmell Beck.

From the Beck turn around and head back to the summit of Scafell Pike via your descent route. Again, with no need to hang about on the summit, descend via your original ascent route and the west spur of Lingmell to the trail coming from Wasdale Head to Lingmell Gill. This is incredible fast and free running.

When you get to the trail coming from Wasdale Head follow it round to the east and the gate next to Lingmell Gill. Once you're through the gate, head back up to Scafell Pike summit via the trail heading east to Mickledore and then north-east to the summit.

Once more, with no need to hang about on the summit, descend via the main tourist trail heading north-west, then south-west via Brown Tongue, and back to the gate at Lingmell Gill – another incredibly fast descent.

From the gate head back to the summit of Scafell Pike via the trail you just descended. This is a last chance for a selfie on the summit before you descend back to the gate via Mickledore.

Looking from the gate across Lingmell Gill towards the banking on the other side, there's an unmarked trail heading steeply up, southwards towards Rakehead Crag and then the summit of Scafell (964m).

To complete the Leg Press you must cross Lingmell Gill at the point close to the gate. Once across the gill, pick up the faint stepped out trail heading steeply south-east towards the red screes and gully on the east shoulder of Rakehead Crag – this is challenging terrain on tired legs.

Negotiate the super-steep hillside to the red screes, and continue through the gully onto the huge shoulder of Scafell. Dig deep, stand tall and breathe as you follow the trail to the east and the final climb to the summit of Scafell (964m).

Feel the full effect of 'The Lakes Leg Press' as you hold one eye on the summit, and press on. From the summit begin your final epic descent via your ascent route back across Lingmell Gill, and directly back into the car park, saving some energy for the demanding red screes.

Chloe Wilson summit sunshine. **Photo**: John Proctor.

North Wales: Snowdon Skyrunner

Welcome to north Wales and the Snowdon skyrunner series. This is a landscape full of myths, legends and folklore, and magical adventures await the skyrunner in this series full of excitement and challenge. Gnarly mountain ridges, rugged rock scrambles and fast track descents; this is world-class running over a diverse and awe-inspiring landscape, and is a great place to hone your skills, and challenge you to perform at your very best.

The series comprises six runs over three mountain ridges, linked together like the contours of a dragon's spine, creating an ancient and mythical Ultra skyline. Awaken the inner King Arthur sleeping deep within your mind, accept the quest, and slay the dragon.

John Proctor aiming for Snowdon, crossing the Glyders. **Photo**: Charlie Proctor.

Ogwen Valley

Ogwen 15
15km | 1950m ascent | max elevation 991m | 3–5 hours

Incredible skyrunning from the very first step, and accessible to all, this is a great run for honing desired skills, or just to become top of your game in your run through the park. This sky run packs in a lot of quality, rugged and gnarly terrain, great rock features and scrambles, ridge running, fast descents and steep climbs – a run to suit all.

The Skyrun
There are many places to park your car on the A5 as you drive into the Ogwen Valley. The run begins directly below the north ridge of Tryfan near the Milestone Buttress parking area, so you should try to park as close to this as possible.

Step through the gate and onto the trail below Milestone Buttress, heading south and up onto the north ridge of Tryfan. After the initial steep ground is gained, staying true to the ridge, you may find one of the 'Cannons' – the first of the rock features.

Continue on upwards, finding the best of the scrambling on the ridgeline, until you summit and find 'Adam and Eve'. Enjoy the exposure as you leap or step from Adam to Eve and back again, then continue over Tryfan's far south peak and descend into the Bwlch Tryfan below Bristly Ridge. >>

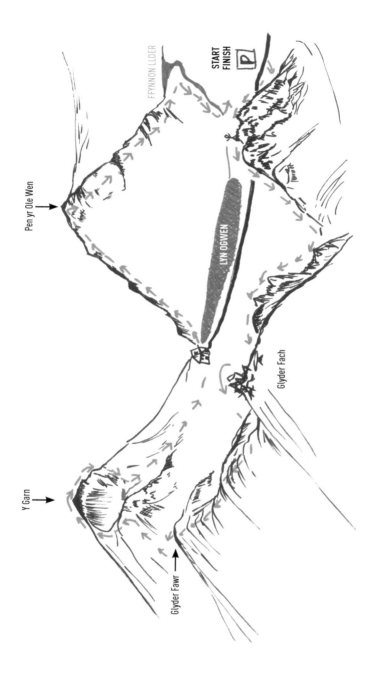

Head up into the lower gullies and aim for the crest as you gain height and cross the pinnacles towards the summit of Glyder Fach (994m). This section presents great exposed scrambling on rough and rugged rock features, high above the valley floor. As the ridge melds into the summit, the 'Cantilever Stone' will appear – another of the amazing rock features on this run.

From the Cantilever Stone head south-west over the impressive jumble of rocks called the Castell y Gwynt and then along the ridge to Glyder Fawr (999m).

There is technical running down the steep screes to Lyn y Cwn – a small lake above the Devil's Kitchen – from where there's a good uphill track heading north-west to Y Garn (947m).

From the summit of Y Garn take the ridge heading north-east for a wonderful fast and free descent all the way to the beach of Llyn Idwal, and then follow the main track down to the visitor centre at Idwal Cottage.

Cross the road heading to the north and begin the climb up Pen yr Ole Wen (978m). This is an unrelenting climb of around 700m, which requires a focused strong pace all the way to the summit. From the summit take the ridge running east, and descend back to the road via the trail running alongside Afon Lloer, a beck flowing out of Fynnon Lloer.

At the road, turn west and head back to your car.

John proctor on the ridgeline. **Photo**: Charlie Proctor.

Carneddau 15

15.5km | 1130m ascent | max elevation 1061m | 3–4 hours

This is ridge running at its finest, high above the valley floor. Your entry is via a 700m steep climb which leads to a blissful run on good tracks over 9km of ridgeline. Never too technical, this run allows you to set a good pace within the peace and tranquillity of the high mountain, well away from the ascending crowds of Mount Snowdon.

The Skyrun

Heading into the Ogwen Valley along the A5 there are many places to park your car. Once you have parked up, head to Idwal Cottage visitor centre for the start of the run.

Cross the road and head north-east alongside the river emerging from the mouth of Llyn Ogwen. Cross over the river where the gate in the wall allows you to pick up the track heading up to Pen yr Ole Wen (978m).

Begin the climb; a strong and steady pace opens the widening panorama as you gain height and head towards the summit. From the summit continue north-east, dropping into Bwlch Carnedd Fach and then head steadily uphill to the summit of Carnedd Dafydd (1044m).

Continue along the ridge Cefn Ysgolion Duo, dropping down to the east through the Bwlch and then to the north as you climb towards the summit of Carnedd Llewelyn (1064m).

Start the descent from the summit via the east ridge; this section gives you good running with some short technical sections as you drop all the way down to Ffynnon Llugwy reservoir and join the fast road back to the A5 and your car.

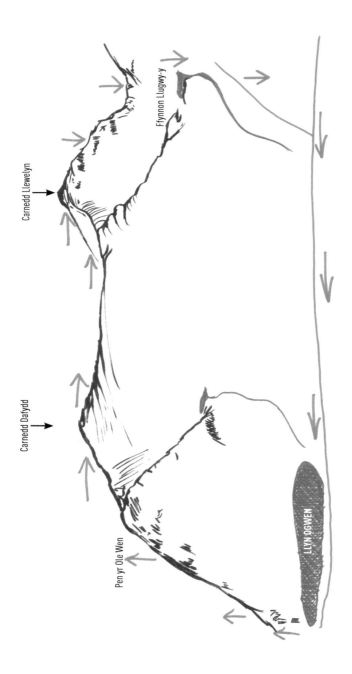

Carnedd Llewelyn

Ffynnon Llugwy-y

Carnedd Dafydd

Pen yr Ole Wen

LLYN OGWEN

Snowdon

Snowdon 20

20km | **1780m ascent** | **max elevation 1079m** | **5–6 hours**

Gnarly and unforgiving skyrunning, this route calls for complete and total focus from the runner. Super-exposed ridge running, delicate and balanced rock scrambling, a huge descent from the summit of Wales' highest peak, heading down over rocky ridgelines and through lush green forest; this is incredible running through a majestic and inspiring mountain landscape.

The Skyrun

Find a parking spot by the Pen y Gwryd Hotel, which is located at the junction of the A498 and A4086 close to Llyn Lockwood.

From your car head south along the A498 (on the right-hand side of the road) to the gate and trail that runs west below the A4086, all the way to the Pen y Pass car park and visitor centre. This is a steady trail to warm you up for the challenging next leg.

Take the trail from the car park, heading west to the junction at the bottom of Crib Goch (there is a sign-posted gate at this point).

Now begin your ascent – steady hill climbing at first, then some steep rock scrambling until you reach the ridge of Crib Goch. Gridlock caused by too many people can be a problem all the way along this ridgeline, so be super careful and aware of others around you and of the line you follow. >>

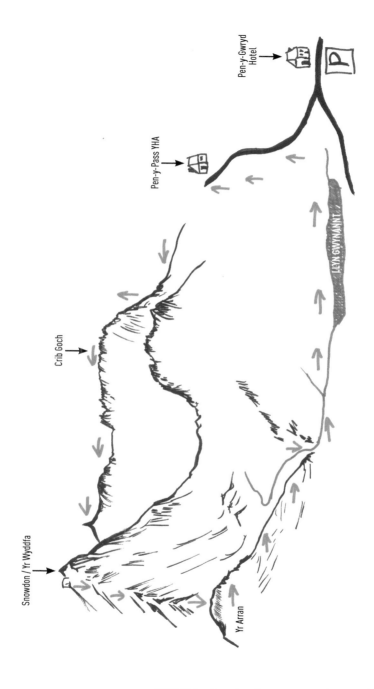

Along the ridge, stay true to the crest for balanced and exposed running on an amazing route. Continue over the pinnacles and head along the trail to the final short scramble and the ascent of Garnedd Ugain (1065m).

Head south-west to the main trail, and the crowds of people aiming upwards to the south-east and the summit of Snowdon (1065m).

From the summit pick up the trail heading south-west, and the descent over the ridgeline that turns to the south and drops to Bwlch Cwm Llan and the lake at the old quarry workings below Yr Arran. A descent of 500m over a 2.5km ridgeline, this is quality, free running which requires total focus for the utmost fun.

From the saddle take the trail heading south for the summit of Yr Arran (747m), a steady twisting trail.

Turning back down the trail to the north-east cross back over the wall and take the trail heading down the ridgeline to the east. When the wall drops away to the south, the trail heads down north-east past some awesome mine-shafts, before descending to the old mine buildings by the ford and track.

Aiming for Llyn Gwynant to the east, head south along the track, dropping down into the valley past some beautiful rock pools and waterfalls. Continue on this trail for about 4km, heading north-east through lush forest as you traverse along the side of Llyn Gwynant, and head up the valley until you come to the waterworks at the bottom of a huge pipeline.

Cross the footbridge and pick up the track heading north below the A498, all the way back to the car.

he Otley Terminator on the lower ridges of Lliwedd. **Photo**: John proctor.

Ogwen-Snowdon Link-up

28km | 2360m ascent | max elevation 1070m | 7–8 hours

This is an exceptional sky run with elements of fast and free running linked by steep rugged rock scrambles, and exposed technical ridges atop of demanding steep ascents. Dig deep within, accept this challenge, head to the horizon and emerge with everlasting memories.

The Skyrun

As for the Ogwen 12K, begin your run below the north ridge of Tryfan, and continue on this route until you ascend out from Bristly Ridge on Glyder Fach. Climb the Cantilever Stone and head over the top of Castell y Gwynt heading west to Glyder Fawr.

From the summit of Glyder Fawr (999m) turn to the trail which heads south and then picks up the spur heading south-east down to the Pen y Pass visitor centre.

From the Pen y Pass take the Miners' Track heading south towards the Llyn Llydaw reservoir. As you approach Llyn Llydaw on the track, take the trail heading south towards Lliwedd Bach and begin your ascent of Lliwedd (898m).

From the summit descend the crest of the ridge, downward climbing above the huge north face; looking beyond this you will see the impressive mountain panorama of Crib Goch and your descent from Snowdon's summit.

Heading north-west pick up the Watkin trail and the climb to the south ridge; once on the ridge head up to the summit of Snowdon (1085m). >>

Descend via the main track heading north for the trail to Garnedd Ugain and the exhilarating west to east descent of Crib Goch.

From the trig point on Garnedd Ugain (1065m) stay true to the ridgeline, a great technical and exposed descent is about to begin. Maintain good balance and posture as you head down to the east, running and downward climbing to the pinnacles and the entry to Crib Goch.

Be aware of the possible carnage along Crib Goch, especially on the steep downward climbing, for many people climb up this route, and there can be gridlock, anguish and cries for help. Be warned: "You are in descent and may step on one."

Find your line through the pinnacles and approach the airy and exhilarating ridge with total focus, awareness and commitment. Cross the ridge and then downward climb to the trail junction at the bottom.

Turn to the east, running fast and free along the trail to the Pen y Pass visitor centre and Youth Hostel.

Cross the road to the left of the Youth Hostel and pick up the trail heading north to Llyn Cwmffynnon; follow the LLyn round to the east, cross the stream by the wall and then head east and traverse to the wall and Miners' Track junction.

Continue steadily up the Miners' Track to the north-east, and the track junction at the head of Cwm Tryfan by Llyn Caseg-Fraith. Although steep at first, heading north-west, your descent through Cwm Tryfan is fast and free, all the way back to the valley and your car.

Ⓜ ⑥ Ogwen Valley Link-up

25km, | **2170m ascent,** | **1050m max elevation** | **7–8 hours**

This presents a classic skyline through rugged and varied terrain, allowing the runner to experience and develop their full range of skyrunning skill sets in a challenging and engulfing mountain environment.

Starting below Tryfan run the Ogwen 12k to the summit of Pen yr Ole Wen (978m) and continue along the Carnedd 24k route all the way back to your car.

view down the Ogwen valley. **Photo:** Lydon Chatting-Walters.

Snowdon Slayer

45km | 3830m ascent | 1040 max elevation | 10–12 hours

A superb skyrun of magnificent variety and commitment, this route incorporates seemingly endless changes of terrain, demanding great skyrunning skills, and mental and physical strength from the runner. Combining all the highlights of the Snowdon series into one epic day, this challenge releases the runner from their everyday norms and constraints into a journey through a magical mountain realm. Step in and summon up your inner-Arthur to run the Snowdon Slayer and complete the Welsh Series.

The skyrun
Park near the Pen y Gwryd Hotel at the junction of the A4086 and A498.

Begin heading south along the right-hand side of the A498 for a short distance to the gate and track running below, then head south down the track to the waterworks and pipeline. **>>**

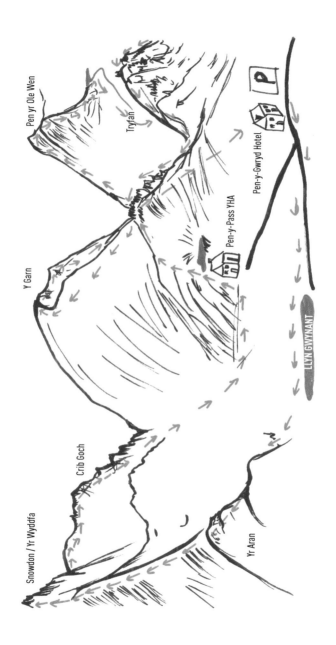

Pen yr Ole Wen

Tryfan

Y Garn

Pen-y-Pass YHA

Pen-y-Gwryd Hotel

LLYN GWYNANT

Crib Goch

Snowdon / Yr Wyddfa

Yr Aran

P

Cross the footbridge near the cottages and head south on the trail downstream and alongside Llyn Gwynant – this is great running all the way through lush woodlands.

Pick up the track heading round to the west, cross the streams where they meet and head up towards the waterfall and rock pools. Cross the slate bridge above the waterfalls and take the track running north up the valley.

After a few hundred meters, the ground levels, and some old mine buildings sit next to the bend in the stream. From here take the trail heading up to the west and begin your ascent of Yr Arran (747m).

You will find steep climbing past some impressive mine shafts until you find the wall on the ridge; follow the wall heading up to the west as far as the stile. Step over the stile and continue south-west up the ridge to the summit.

From the summit reverse the trail back to the stile then continue north-west heading down to Bwlch Cwm Llan by the old mines.

From Bwlch Cwm Llan continue north and begin your ascent of Snowdon's south ridge – this is impressive ridge running, and continued focus and a steady pace is required. Follow the ridge round to the north-east and the summit of Snowdon (1085m).

Head down from the summit via the main track heading north, and then head upwards to the north-east and the trail to Garnedd Ugain (1065m).

From the summit begin your descent of one of the finest sections of skyrunning in this series, for the west to east traverse of Crib Goch requires a high level of skyrunning skills and is undoubtably a moment of intense pleasure and joy.

Again, be aware of the possible carnage along Crib Goch, especially on the steep downward climbing, for many people climb up this route, and there can be gridlock, anguish and cries for help. Be warned: "You are in descent and may step on one."

Find your line through the pinnacles, and approach the airy and exhilarating ridge with total focus, awareness and commitment. Cross the ridge and then downward climb to the trail junction at the bottom.

Turn to the east, running fast and free along the trail to the Pen y Pass visitor centre and Youth Hostel.

Cross the road to the left of the Youth Hostel and pick up the trail heading north to Llyn Cwmffynnon following the LLyn round to the east, cross the stream and head to the wall and Miners' Track junction.

Steadily continue up the Miners' Track to the north-east and the track junction at the head of Cwm Tryfan. (Take note – the descent back down the Miners' Track all the way to the A498 is your route back to your car.)

As for the Ogwen 12k, continue your east to west traverse of the Glyders and then descend into the Ogwen valley before making the superbly challenging climb up to the summit of Pen yr Ole Wen (978m).

From the summit of Pen yr Ole Wen, continue the route as described for the Ogwen 12k, head east down the spur, and pick up the trail running alongside Afon Lloer. Descend into the Ogwen valley and continue up and over Tryfan and then on to Bristly Ridge and the summit area of Glyder Fach.

Turning down to the east, leave the summit area via the trail running to the Miners' Track. Heading south, follow the trail descending all the way back to your car near the Pen y Gwryd Hotel – a wonderful trail on tired legs.

Alternative start

You may want to consider starting this sky run by parking in the Ogwen valley below Tryfan, in order to be fresh for the technical scrambling on Bristly Ridge. However, if you wish to complete the Skylander Ultra in Scotland, tackling Bristly Ridge at the end of a big day will be good training for that event.

Bonus sections

As you cross the Glyders, having already completed the Ogwen 12k, you may want to consider tackling one of two extra options for the descent into the Ogwen valley.

1   Y Gribin

Heading west from Glyder Fach to Glyder Fawr you will see the north facing ridgeline of Y Gribin. This is an excellent steep and technical descent with some downward climbing and a fast track to Ogwen Cottage, and requires absolute focus.

2   Devil's Kitchen

Having dropped down the screes to Llyn Cwm from the summit of Glyder Fawr (999m), a trail heading to the north descends through the head wall of Cwm Idwal. Known as the Devil's Kitchen, this is a descent through impressive rock formations to fast and free sublime running through Cwm Idwal to Ogwen Cottage.

Fast and free, John Proctor focused on descent through the Devils Kitchen. **Photo**: Charlie Poctor.

Rhitta *'The fearsome Giant of Snowdon'*

51km | **3250m ascent** | **1040 max elevation** | **8–12 hours**

Bonus Skyrun

This is a true test of endurance! Begin by parking near the Pen y Gwryd Hotel at the junction of the A4086 and A498.

Heading south, cross the A498 and take the trail running alongside and down to the works and cottages below the huge pipeline.

Cross the bridge onto the trail running south to south-west past Llyn Gwynant, and then begin heading up to the west until you are above the waterfalls at the ford by the old ruins.

Heading south-west, begin your ascent of Yr Aran via its east ridge; from the summit, head to the north and drop down to the saddle by the old quarries before heading up the south ridge of Snowdon all the way to the summit (1085m).

Leave the summit, and head north-west along the main track to the Rangers' Path, heading down to the west above the awesome cliffs of Clogwyn Du'r Arddu. Descend to the reservoir, Llyn Ffynnon y gwas.

Heading south from Llyn Ffynnon y gwas, pick up the small reservoir in Cwm Treweunydd. From here begin your second ascent of Snowdon by heading south across rough flat ground, and then south-east to begin the climb. Head for the rising ridgeline and the Rhyd Ddu path taking you back onto the main ridgeline and the summit of Snowdon. >>

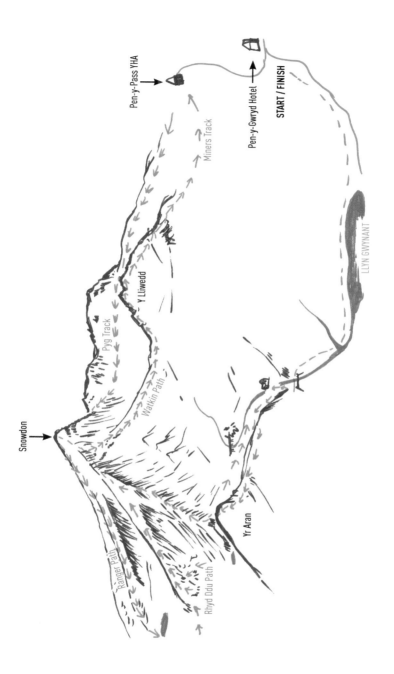

Pen-y-Pass YHA

Miners Track

Snowdon

Pyg Track

Y Lliwedd

Watkin Path

Ranger Path

Rhyd Ddu Path

Yr Aran

Pen-y-Gwryd Hotel

START / FINISH

LLYN GWYNANT

From the summit descend via the Watkin path heading south-east, and continue over the peaks of Y Lliwedd descending the trail to the north and to the Llyn Llydaw reservoir. From the reservoir continue along the Miners Track to the Pen y Pass.

From the pass, heading to the west take the Pyg Track all the way back to the summit of Snowdon for your third and final ascent of the mountain.

From the summit, head back down the south ridge to Bwlch Cwm Llan below Yr Aran. From the Bwlch take the trail heading east back down past the old mines until you drop down past the waterfalls and continue along the trail, heading to the north-east, past Llyn Gwynant and up the valley back to your car.

Rich Allen on the ridges – Rhitta. photo. **Photo:** John Proctor.

Scotland: Highland Skyrunner

Welcome to the west coast and the Highland skyrunner series of this guide. Great freedom and honour await the driven and disciplined soul, beckoned by vision and dreams. This is a territory of big skies, gnarly landscapes and ferocious weather.

Encompass the highly dramatic north face of the Ben, and descend from its majestic magnificence, a wonder from the power of creation. Breathe deep as you stride airily across the ridges of Steal and take great strength from your commitment as you meet the skies of Glencoe.

The rewards are high for those who are able to overcome, and for those, who may one day arrive at their summit, this is a final peak, and the UK's ultimate sky run:

'The Skylander, for there is challenge beyond.'

John Proctor on the Skylander. **Photo**: John Proctor.

The Ben 15

15km | 1324m ascent | max elevation 1080m | 3–5 hours

An exhilarating and awe-inspiring run over Britain's highest and most dramatic peak, this is an epic mountain climb and ridge run to the summit with an 'eyes wide-open' descent through the mighty rock walls and ridges of the iconic north face.

The Skyrun

Park up at the sign-posted North Face car park, just off the A82 for the start of this sky run.

Take the North Face trail heading up through the woodland and onto the main trail heading south-east towards the Charles Inglis Clark (CIC) memorial hut. This is a hard start to the day, going through the woods; exit them onto the main trail and ascend at a good pace until you are surrounded by the amphitheatre of the Ben, and arrive close to the CIC hut.

From the CIC hut, turn to the north and begin a rising traverse with rugged ground underfoot to reach the summit of Carn Beag Dearg (1010m).

Heading south-east, cast your eyes thoughtfully towards the mighty North Face and identify its huge distinctive features: the Observatory Ridge and Buttress, Tower Ridge, Coire na Ciste, the Trident and Carn Dearg. Your descent down the Ledge Route begins on Carn Dearg and drops down the ridge to Carn Dearg Butress.

Stride with a good pace over the Carn Dearg Meadhonach and Carn Mor Dearg, excellent ridge running all the way. Drop down to the south and across the Carn Mor Dearg Arête until you join the main mass of Ben Nevis. >>

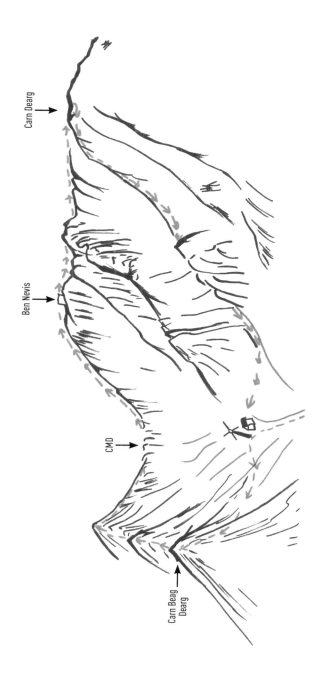

Carn Dearg

Ben Nevis

CMD

Carn Beag
Dearg

Continue heading up towards the west and the summit of Ben Nevis.

Carefully navigate your way off the summit towards Carn Dearg (1214m
along the top of Coire na Ciste. For your descent of the Ledge Route, pick up
the ridge and follow it down to the main Buttress; look out for the pinnacle
block and broad terrace and continue your descent of the Ledge Route, and
then the trail back to the CIC hut. Embrace the magnificence of this environ
ment and stand tall over the sustained technical running, maintaining grea
focus and balance.

Once you arrive at the CIC hut, soak up the atmosphere one last time befor
you turn down to the north-west and begin the fast and free run all the wa
back to the car. This is a wonderful trail on which you can maintain a goo
pace as you soak up the last of the day.

Johon Proctor at the top of Ledge route. **Photo:** John Proctor.

Glencoe Skyrun

27km | 3600m ascent | max elevation 1125m | 10–12 hours

Widely recognised for its distinctive features and excellence, this iconic sky run is a rock 'n' roller-coaster ride, demanding superstar levels of skill and endurance. Traverse the pinnacle ridge of Aonach Eagach, climb the classic Curved Ridge on the Buachaille and run the fortress massif of Bidean nam Bian. This route presents iconic running through outstanding natural beauty, and is a real superstar of the skyrunning world. Take to the stage, and become the Rock Star.

The Skyrun

Begin by parking in the car park next to Loch Achtriochtan alongside the A82 at the west end of Glen Coe.

Heading north, cross the A82 and begin your climb of Sgorr nam Fiannaidh (967m), initially via the spur running along Allt an t-Sidhein, and then over steep rough ground to the summit. Recover from the climb as you head east on steady ground to Stob Coire Leith (940m).

Heading into the rising sun, continue along the Aonach Eagach, enjoying this fine position. Stay focused as the exposure engulfs your movement along the notches, pinnacles and knife-edge ridgelines until the final climb onto Am Bodach.

Putting the pinnacles behind you, continue heading east along the broadening ridgeline to Sron Garbh (873m), and carry on running the ridgeline until your descent to the Devil's Staircase via Stob Mhic Mhartuin (707m) – this is fine running through an open and breathtaking landscape. >>

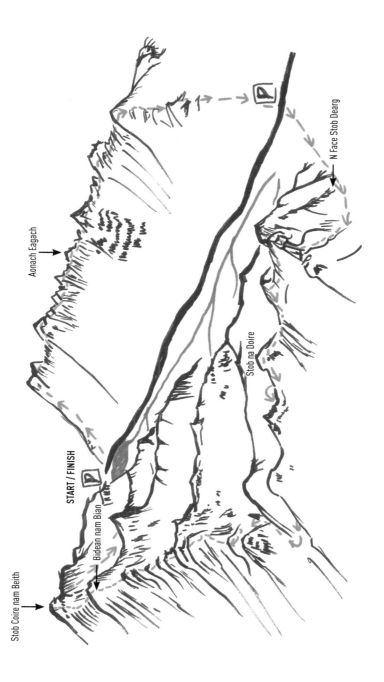

Stob Coire nam Beith

Aonach Eagach

N Face Stob Dearg

Stob na Doire

START / FINISH

Bidean nam Bian

Take the Devil's Staircase heading down to the south, cross the A82 and continue along the trail running below the mighty north face of Stob Dearg to the rock scramble on Curved Ridge. Ascend the rising ridgeline below the drama of Rannoch Wall and rise above the wild eastern expanse of Rannoch Moor a truly awesome scramble in an astonishing and mind-blowing situation.

Heading west then south-west from the summit of Stob Dearg (1022m continue across the ridge of Buachaille Etive Mor over Stob na Doire (1011m and descend into the saddle below Stob Coire Altrum for the fast and fre descent heading down to the north into Lairig Gartain.

Heading south-west along the Lairig Gartain, cross the saddle between Sto na Broige and Stob Dubh and descend to the trail contouring around Sto Dubh's south ridge, on to the trail heading north and up to Lairig Eilde.

Follow the trail to the large cairn situated on the saddle between Stob Dub and Stob Coire Sgreamhach.

Heading to the south-west begin your ascent of Stob Coire Sgreamhac (1072m) and the traverse of Bidean nam Bian, a demanding and exhilaratin ridge run.

From the cairn head up over rough ground to the small saddle below spo height 778, a small peak on the south east shoulder of Stob Coire Sgreamhac

Continue heading north-west over the summit and along the ridgeline Bidean nam Bian (1150m).

From Bidean nam Bian a great trail, via Stob Coire nam Beith (1107m) and bealac An t-Sron, heads down through impressive rock architecture into Glenco This is incredibly fast and technical running all the way to the car.

Greg Boswell technical ridge running in the dramatic surroundings of Glen Coe. **Photo**: Hamish Frost.

Ring of Steall

14.8km | 1532m ascent | max elevation 1080m | 4–6 hours

'... along with the forests and forest belonging to the said earth ...'
Lord Gordon – in the grant of Lochaber to Alexander (1500)

**Feel the true and primeval spirit of your very soul as you run by the waters
of Ben Nevis through the remnants of an ancient Caledonian woodland.
Dig deep for an epic lung-busting climb to a ridgeline high in the sky, then
tip-toe or dance along the ridge of the Devil before the final summit and an
exhilarating descent directly back to your start line. Awaken the hidden
soul deep within, on this unmissable run through the skies of our ancestors**

The Skyrun

Begin by parking at the Polldubh Falls car park in Glen Nevis.

Head across the bridge over the waterfalls and continue along the road heading east alongside the River Nevis; then leave the road and move onto the
trail, continuing east – a good warm up for your legs.

The trail becomes technical, turning to the south-east along the edge of a
great gorge, with the possibility of encountering many hikers along the way.

A classic view of Steall Falls appears as you leave the gorge and head into the
open Glen and the cable bridge crossing the River Nevis. Cross the bridge and
head under the Falls close to its base, continuing over boggy ground until the
trail turns north-east and begins the steep ascent of An Gearanach (982m).
This is a steady climb, which due to its zig-zagging nature allows for a strong
and sustained effort; remain focused until the last steps onto the summit. **>>**

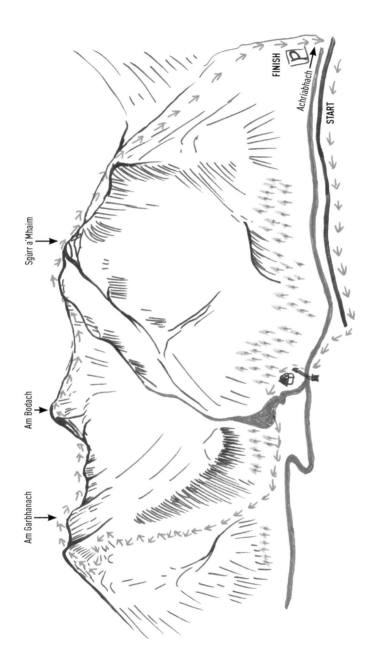

FINISH

START

Achriabhach

Sgùrr a 'Mhaim

Am Bodach

Am Garbhanach

Head to the south along the excellent ridgeline connecting An Garbhanach Stob Coire a Chairn and Am Bodach (1032m). This is ridge running at its finest with fast and technical running until the short scramble onto Am Bodach summit. Descend via the west ridge to the saddle below Sgurr an Iubhair, and continue to its summit.

Descend via the north ridge, heading to Stob Choire a Mhail and Sgurr a Mhaim (1099m) via the Devil's Ridge. This is incredibly wild and exposed ridge running requiring total focus and commitment.

From the summit of Sgurr a Mhaim, descend the very fast and free, rock north-west ridge onto the trail heading through the fence and back to you car. This is a real leg-busting descent with the cold crystal waters of the rive to soothe and cool down in at the end.

Greg Boswell heading up to the ridge. **Photo:** Hamish Frost.

The Skylander

58km | 5281m ascent | max elevation 1335m | 15 hours

Welcome to the Skylander, an epic sky run across an unrelenting, wildly exposed and ancient landscape. Only the truly committed and self-actualised skyrunner will succeed; linking together the highlights of the three great sky runs in this chapter, this is an Ultra born of great love and desire, and comes second to none. It is indeed a worthy contender for being one of the greatest UK-wide sky runs.

The following is a word on my experience when setting off on the Skylander *'There's a coldness in the air and all is quiet on the mountain; the first rays of sunshine open up the mighty and majestic north face of Ben Nevis as it breaks cover from the darkness. Engulfed by incredible feelings of strength, excitement and desire, billions of neurons light up the inner mind. I tune into the atmosphere, step forward into the day, and drift deeper into my soul; the trail has begun, time's rolling on'.* >>

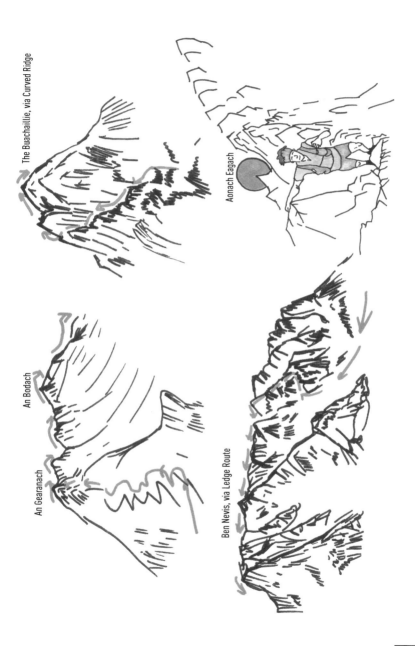

The Buachaillie, via Curved Ridge

Aonach Eagach

An Bodach

An Gearanach

Ben Nevis, via Ledge Route

The skyrun

Beginning at the North Face car park below Ben Nevis and ending up belo
Aonach Eagach's west peak Sgorr nam Fiannaidh, this is the only run in th
series to finish at a different location from the starting point. If you have tw
cars, then drop one of them in the small car park close to Loch Achtriochta
in Glencoe. However, if you are on your own, as I was on this run, I wou
suggest pitching a tent close to the end of the route and leave a sleeping ba
there, along with your recovery food etc. You can then hitch-hike or arrang
a taxi back to the North Face car park.

Park up at the North Face car park and begin your day, early with the first ray
of light, by heading for the Ledge Route on the Ben's North Face. Early-seaso
runners, beware – verglas can cover the slab of rock that is climbed to acce
the route. Ascend the Ledge Route, enjoying the drama of the North Fac
and the fine position in which you find yourself. From the summit of Car
Dearg, head up towards the summit of Ben Nevis.

Heading south-east, carefully descend to the CMD arête and continue to th
summit of Carn Mor Dearg, along wonderful ridge running in an epic locatio
From the summit, turn to the east and descend the ridgeline to the head
Coire Giubhsachan, then turning to the south, follow the water course an
run fast and free all the way to the waters of the Nevis river and the valle
floor. Cross the river either by wading through it, or, if in any doubt about th
water flow, take the wire bridge further down the river.

Once across the river begin the climb up to An Gearanach, and continue fro
the summit, striding the brow across the ridgeline heading to Am Bodac
Head down the west ridge from the summit to Coire na h-Eirghe, then pic
up the decent trail all the way to Kinlochleven.

From the village pick up the track behind the Ice Factor (Ice Climbing and Mountain Activity Centre), and then head along the sign-posted West Highland Way and run to the A82 and the Buachaillie; this is a steady section of running that allows time for some recovery and refuelling. Cross the A82 and head to the north face of Stob Dearg for your ascent of Curved Ridge – a wonderful ridge scramble in a majestic position, giving incredible views all the way to the summit and beyond.

From the summit of Stob Dearg follow the trail to the head of Coire na Tulaich and then descend through the Coire heading north back to the A82. Cross the road, turn to the west, and continue along the roadside being aware of the fast-approaching traffic. There is a trail along the roadside, which you can follow to the abandoned building known as Allt na Reigh. From behind the building you can begin your ascent of Am Bodach (943m) – the final big climb of the run, and the entrance to the incredible Aonach Eagach ridge.

Tired and worn out, ensure you nevertheless approach the final balancing act with focused commitment: a fine day comes to a close as you cross the ridgeline and head into the setting sun.

As you approach the final climb of the ridge to Sgorr nam Fiannaidh (967m), there is a small saddle from which you can begin your descent to the south and down to the road. If you are not 100 per cent sure of this descent, you must continue to the summit and begin your descent from there.

It's a brutal descent on tired legs.

Once back down at the roadside, breathe deep and enjoy your achievement: it's been a big day.

Glencoe. **Photo**: Hamish Frost.

Helping hands and kind words

There's a great bunch of folk who have helped to create this guideboo[
the proof runners; the artists and most of all; Bernadette Cook, aka *Bx E*
for the words that got me hooked. I've included contact details and a bri[
description of their skills should you wish to contact them.

Andy Swann
'Enjoyed this immensely'

The "Grit father" a rock athlete of commitment and distinction, a mountain/climbir
coach offering technical climbing and movement skills. Instagram: *@climb-for-life1*

Iain Taylor
'made me want to put my running legs on'

Coming from the people's republic of Batley, a truly old school Fells Man, a winter
Bod Graham runner, university lecturer and outdoor educator.

Jessica Richardson
'I'm so excited to get proofing the routes'

A Fells Women, heading into motherhood, the Bob Graham & Paddy Buckly in her
shadow. A mountain leader offering navigation and hill skills, she even hires campe[
vans to folk. Instagram: *@dinkycamperhire*

Andrew Sugden
'The rocks up to Scafell Pike from Esk Hause are lethal in the wet'

Last seen heading into the unknown after the Lakes in a Day, a teacher
of the sciences and above all, a Fells Men.

Rich Allen, AKA 'T Otley Terminator'
'Looks ace, Wainwright-esq'

A teacher of geography, a finisher of the marathon des sables, a gear freak who loves
a review. Instagram: *@climbinggearreviews*

Becky James
'Thanks for inviting me to contribute'

Artist Becky promotes traditional ways of life through her website, please go to:
carryforthtradition.com. She also practices Falun Dafa *en.falundafa.org* and is an
activist raising awareness about the ongoing persecution of this peaceful Buddhist
meditation practice, she aims to end organ tourism to China through the website:
endtransplantabuse.org

Clarke Butler
'you're welcome. I enjoyed doing it'

EX Royal Marine Commander, a mountaineering and climbing skills coach,
an awesome portrait sketcher should you like one. Instagram: *@remoteoptions*

Matt Bibbings
'I'll give it a crack for sure'

Family man, DIY dad, adventure pursuits instructor, mountain biker, master of
the waterways and graphics genius.

Majka Bajika
'Wow!!! Keep going'

Wildly strong, a forensic psychiatrist at Tranter, with Etive, Rigby and Ramsey in her shadow.

Hamish Frost
'yeah of course, no bother'

Awesome mountain and adventure sports photographer, true gentleman and always in the right place at the right time. Instagram: *@hamishfrost.com*

Rachel Duncan
'I've very much enjoyed working on this project'

A freelance proofreader and well-travelled mother who has been trained by the Chartered Institute of Editing and Proofreading. If you like the words in this guide you can check out her Instagram: *@duncanproofreading.com*

Many thanks to all of you.
John Proctor.

Opposite: John Proctor enjoying the finer side of life, surrounded by the Patagonia landscape. **Photo**: Paul Reeve.

About the Author

John Proctor is an adventure pursuits athlete who believes in the spiritual and physical characteristics of the human experience. A holder of the Mountain Climber Instructor Certificate, he enjoys challenge, adventure and spending days in the mountain environment helping others discover self believe through adventure.

runner, alpinist and rock climber who has exceeded his own expectations through self-belief and trying things that could be deemed beyond him. Whilst on a recent climbing holiday in Patagonia he took on a solo speed ascent of the remote mountain Cerro Huemul, a 46 km run with 3200m ascent. One of his most memorable ascents in the Alps, came while climbing The Cassin; a classic 800m route on the North face of the Piz Badile. It was his wife Anna's 30th birthday and they were climbing with close friends who were on their honeymoon.

e wrote this guide to help inspire runners and climbers take up the challenge of skyrunning and offer adventure away from the traditional mountain running rounds.

ohn can be contacted for personal guiding and skills development through *reakcliffe@googlemail.com*, or on Instagram: *@Big-Friend-Academy*

ou can book skyrunning courses through: *www.lakelandsummits.com* r canyoning and other adventures through: *ww.yorkshireadventurecompany.co.uk*

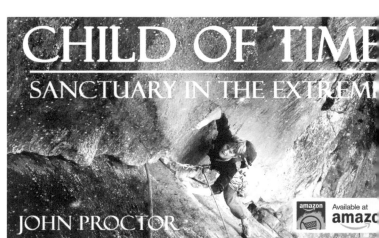

CHILD OF TIME

SANCTUARY IN THE EXTREME

JOHN PROCTOR

The life of a climber, simple in need, rich in experience

"A powerful and inspiring story of one mans journey into the world of climbing and mountaineering which ultimatley saved him from a downward spiral of violence and criminality"

"...free-wheeling, reckless, headbanging and danger-encrusted."